Help Your Child With Homoeopathy

SHEILA HARRISON RGN

Help Your Child With
Homoeopathy

ASHGROVE PRESS, BATH

First published in Great Britain by
ASHGROVE PRESS LIMITED
4 Brassmill Centre, Brassmill Lane
Bath BA1 3JN

and distributed in the USA by
Avery Publishing Group Inc.
350 Thorens Avenue
Garden City Park
New York 11040

ISBN 1 85398 008 0

First published 1989

British Library Cataloguing in Publication Data

Harrison, Sheila
    Help your child with homoeopathy
    1. Children. Homoeopathy. Remedies
    I. Title
    615.5'32
ISBN 1-85398-008-0

Photoset by Ann Buchan (Typesetters), Middlesex
Printed and bound in Great Britain by
Dotesios Printers, Bradford on Avon, Wiltshire

Contents

Note

Information on the dosages and
potencies of remedies discussed in
this book will be found on pages
93 and 94.

Preface

I have written this book mainly with parents in mind but also for anyone who has the care of children: nurses, nannies, paramedics and even doctors who have never used homoeopathy but would like to try it out in their practice. I have tried to interpret the rather old fashioned descriptions of symptoms in the homoeopathic language into the language of today. Many homoeopathic books use rather archaic descriptions, and anybody coming new to the discipline may find them difficult to relate to present day experiences.

I will probably come in for some criticism from the classical Hahnemannian homeopaths, so will say now in my defence that I have found in practice that the methods recommended here have been very successful over the years. I do not feel that allopathic (conventional) medicine has no place, as there are certainly times when it is necessary to resort to drugs or surgery; but I do believe that a very high percentage of childrens' ailments are better treated by natural medicines.

Children respond very well to homoeopathy as it shortens the duration of their illnesses and they bounce back to health very quickly. It has an advantage over herbal medicine in that the remedies are pleasant to take. I have never yet met a child who refuses to take homoeopathic remedies.

There are many useful and frequently used childrens' remedies apart from those mentioned in this book, but I have confined myself here to the ones that I have found most consistently valuable, in order to keep this book within reasonable limits. I hope it will encourage those using it to read more comprehensive books on the subject;

you will find a number of them in the section on further reading, as well as useful addresses.

I have kept the introduction as simple as possible in order that newcomers to the discipline will not have difficulty in grasping the basic principles. I hope I have made this book enjoyable to read and whetted your appetite for further study in the future.

Introduction

What is homoeopathy, does it work, how does it work? These questions are asked because, to most people, homoeopathy is a mystery. Well, homoeopathy is a system of medicine very different from the orthodox system which is in common use today. Orthodox treatment usually relies upon giving an illness a name (the diagnosis), and then offering the patient manufactured synethetic drugs designed to relieve the symptoms of the illness, assuming that if the symptoms disappear, the illness has gone. Because of the powerful effects that these drugs have on the systems of the body, it is not surprising that unpleasant side effects are often produced; sometimes more drugs are then given to deal with the side effects.

In modern medicine, if a patient gets a cold the symptoms can be somewhat relieved by nasal decongestants, by antibiotics to prevent the cold 'going to the chest', by anaesthetic throat lozenges to relieve the sore throat. The cold still takes a week to get better because the body needs time to heal itself.

If the patient develops high blood pressure, modern drugs will bring it down, but only as long as they are continually taken. The modern medicine of the pharmaceutical manufacturer does not get rid of the cause.

The principles of homoeopathy are entirely different. Firstly, the correct medicine is that which, if given in large doses to a healthy individual, would actually give that person the symptoms the patient is suffering from. Homoeopathy sees the symptoms only as the body's way of showing that there is something wrong inside, and also as a useful guide to the choice of remedy. Secondly, the more dilute the remedy, the more powerful is its effect. It is

9

this second principle of homoeopathy that many people find difficult to understand, and yet is quite simple. In illness, the body's energies are upset and this often shows as tiredness. We 'haven't much energy' we say. Homoeopathy works by stimulating the body's energies to become normal. When homoeopathic medicines are prepared, more energy goes into making the more dilute remedies, and so they are more powerful.

This system of treatment was discovered by a German doctor, Samuel Hahnemann, nearly 200 years ago. He noticed that people who took quinine developed symptoms of malaria, so treated people who were suffering from malaria with quinine in very diluted doses prepared in a certain way and found that this method cured the disease quickly and without side effects.

Fascinated by the results, he persuaded his healthy students to act as guinea pigs and tried out herbs and other substances in quite substantial doses. He found of course that they developed symptoms of overdosing. These symptoms were listed and compiled into what is known as the Materia Medica, and he called them drug pictures.

Then Hahnemann began to treat patients who presented a set of symptoms with the medicine which corresponded with the drug pictures. An example of this is the common cold with the particular symptoms [drug pictures] of streaming eyes and sneezing. A homoeopathic potency of Allium Cepa – the common onion – helped cure the cold quickly.

However, the common cold does not always have these particular symptoms, so Allium Cepa will not cure all colds. For instance thick green catarrh will call for Pulsatilla (the Wind Flower), while the streaming cold which burns the skin round the nose and upper lip would call for White Arsenic.

We now see that the 'particular' symptoms are very important in choosing the correct remedy. The name of the disease is not important but the particular symptoms are if you are to find the correct remedy for the patient.

It is possible to find medical practitioners who practise homoeopathy, but you are more likely to find that your homoeopath is not medically qualified, but is a 'lay' practitioner who has studied homoeopathy as an art. Your lay practitioner will probably have had a scientific training or have been a para-medic, perhaps a nurse. He will ask you questions which you may think very odd, such as whether you have hot or cold feet, your likes and dislikes, what kind of weather you prefer and your personality traits.

Having said all that, there are remedies that have an affinity with certain organs of the body. For example Lycopodium (Club Moss) and Cheledonium (The Greater Celandine) have an affinity for the liver, may be given to normalise its action even without a full case history, and will do a lot of good.

If you want to treat your child with homoeopathy, what do you do? Well, first of all make a careful note of all the symptoms, write them down, and then if the child is old enough ask a few questions, but be careful how you phrase the questions, as very often a child will give you the answer it thinks you want. For instance, don't ask if the throat feels hot if the child has a sore throat; much better to ask it to describe how it feels. If the child has difficulty giving a description, offer choices. For example, does it feel dry or raw or hot. This way you will get a clearer set of symptoms when choosing your remedy.

Some remedies, as you will see, have some symptoms which are the same, so look for something different about them. As an example, two remedies may have the symptoms of throat dry and burning, but one of these remedies may have thirst as a prominent feature, whilst the other may have thirstlessness, and so on. Not all symptoms may match exactly, but with your list in front of you get the best match you can. Do remember that if you get it wrong you will have done no harm by giving an odd dose of the wrong remedy in a low potency. You will find information on potencies in the chapter on TIPS.

You will notice that some remedies keep re-appearing in this book, sometimes being used for different diseases. If you have not come across homoeopathy before this will seem rather strange. The reason they do is that the drug picture of every remedy is pages long in the Materia Medica, and is divided into sections on different parts of the body, along with a list of symptoms for each one. Thus if we are dealing with sore throats, the remedy symptoms in this book will basically be the symptoms given in the Materia Medica for sore throats, with a few added symptoms from the rest of the drug picture to make choosing the remedy easier.

At this stage you might feel like putting this book away in a drawer. *Don't!* Homoeopathy is an art rather than a science, so be observant and you will get quite skilful at it.

Try to observe adults and children even when they are not ill. You will notice all kinds of things – colouring, stance, extroversion, introversion; whether they respond to sympathy or affection, or whether it aggravates them; whether they are brighter at certain times of the day or whether their symptoms get worse, and so on. You will be surprised what you will see. Go to it. You have nothing to lose and everything to gain.

1
Constitutions and Constitutional Types

CONSTITUTIONS

Most families will have observed that different members have different constitutions. By that I mean that they have certain weaknesses and strengths. The weaknesses in the constitution are the sites in the body where things are likely to go wrong, often referred to as target organs. For example, Tommy is chesty, Ann has rashes, Daddy always has indigestion, Mother is prone to insomnia, and so on.

Our constitution is inherited and determined by the genetic mix at the time of conception, which is why all the members of a family are not alike and their targets are not necessarily the same, although some might be.

Certain diseases from which our ancestors suffered affect our genetic structure which is then passed on from generation to generation. The best time to effect alterations is in infancy when the organism can be modified to some extent with homoeopathy.

I shall give you some information on the four main genetic types which will help you to see which category your child falls into. Naturally, it is unusual for there to be only one type in one person, although one type is usually predominant. It is therefore the predominant type which will cause the most trouble, or to put it another way, the diseases that go with the predominant

13

type of constitution are likely to be the ones that your child suffers from.

Personalities also fall into these four types. When trying to fit your child into a constitutional type it is easier to think back to what they were like in the first two or three years of life, as suppressions by allopathic drugs may have altered the way they manifest their symptoms and personalities.

As you read the constitutional types you will start to notice things you never thought had any significance. If you have difficulty, make lists and you will see one is longer than the others, and there you have your predominant type.

If you find all this too confusing, don't be in a hurry. Notice things over a period of weeks and then try again, and you will be surprised how much easier it is.

Although the information I have given you is not essential in treating your child, it will help you to understand why your child is prone to certain diseases, and will also help you to understand the individual you are dealing with.

CONSTITUTIONAL TYPES

TYPE 1 (Carbo Nitrogenoid)

This type of child is usually intelligent but tires easily from mental and physical exertion. Restless and always on the move they tire themselves out and must lie down. Sensitivity to cold is very marked and the child needs to be kept warm. All symptoms are worse during the day, no matter what the complaint, with improvement towards the evening.

There is a vivid imagination with fear of the dark and

imaginary things, also a tendency to become easily upset by small things. Anxiety with anticipation that things are going to go wrong for them is also common. Quick and fluent in speech, they seem very bright and quick on the uptake. They do however have difficulty in sustaining concentration, and will flit from one thing to another.

There is a marked sensitivity to bright light and noise, both of which in the extreme can make them sick. In appearance they have a triangular face like an inverted pyramid, with medium to small ears. The skin tends to be dry and can appear grubby looking. Very often they are not keen on washing, probably because it makes the skin feel even drier. They are prone to dry scales in the ears, pimples, and polyps in the nose.

The complexion tends to be pale or even sallow, with faint bluish rings round the eyes; the fontanelles in babies are late in closing. The head seems a bit large for the body, with a tendency to sweat and damp the pillow.

Headaches are generally frontal or at the temples and there is an inclination to vertigo. The scalp tends to be dry with dandruff and the hair is difficult to comb when it is dry.

There is a preference for hot foods, fried foods and foods with lots of flavouring in them. They crave sweets, acid and sour foods and particularly like unsuitable things to eat when they are ill. Always hungry, especially in the late morning. Their symptoms are often worse after eating.

There is a tendency to diarrhoea, particulary first thing in the morning. Alternatively, constipation with small hard dry stools alternating with loose stools and a good deal of wind is common, as is nervous diarrhoea from anticipation of some distressing event.

The appetite is precarious as they feel full very quickly after eating, which is why they are always hungry. Sweets of course are so popular because they don't make them feel so full and yet they quickly satisfy the urgent need for calories.

Coughs are usually of the dry, tickling variety, often an allergic cough. Hay fever and dust and hair allergies always have their basis in the Type 1 constitution. Standing for any length of time is impossible for anyone of this constitution, they must lean on something or preferably sit down. Weak ankles can be a problem too and they will often crack when walking.

TYPE 2 (Oxygenoid)

This child is usually hot and prefers a cool atmosphere. It will want to take off its coat or jumper to play out on a cool day. All symptoms are worse at night and improve towards early morning. It is possible for there to be structural problems too, such as poor dental structure and nasal bones. More rarely there will be club toes, bent spine and faulty hip joints; in fact any malformation of the skeleton belongs to this category.

The child tends to be a slow developer both mentally and physically, and can at times be lazy, sulky, suspicious and obstinate. Comprehension is difficult so the child will go over its lessons time and time again before getting a grasp of the subject. It is not a very talkative type and tends to appear phlegmatic.

Restlessness at night is the norm, with a tendency to keep getting up in the night because it just can't settle down. Once this child gets an idea into its head no argument, however reasonable, will shift it. There is a preference for being alone, or at least not joining in, and the child is always wanting to do something, but doesn't know what.

Physically the head will be large, with a greasy skin which is somewhat pale. The ears are large and the lips thicker than those of the other types, with a tendency to split. The nails are thin and the hair rather greasy.

Headaches come on at night and will normally be on the

top of the head or slightly towards the back, with a feeling of coldness in the body. There is a tendency to rub the head into the pillow when sleeping. This type of child is aggravated by warmth, overexertion. They are poor travellers.

The sense of smell may be impaired by snuffles in the nose which form greenish crusts. There may be deformed teeth with constant teething troubles, spongy gums and mouth ulcers.

Inveterate cases of tonsillitis and adenoids belong to this type, with the tonsils being permanently enlarged and hard.

The child will usually have a good appetite even when ill, and especially likes cold food and drinks. Not very keen on meat, it will sometimes refuse it altogether. Coughs are barking.

There is sometimes pain in the long bones of the body which seem to be affected by changes in the weather, especially cold and damp. These must not be confused with muscular pains.

Skin problems tend to be located behind the knee, the crook of the elbow or in places where there are folds in the skin.

The eruptions are grouped in rings or may be single circular patches. The skin problems of this type seem to cause very little distress, with no itching, although they may look raw and have a brownish cast.

TYPE 3 (Tubercular)

Type 3 is a combination of Types 1 and 2, so the characteristics of both these types are present together.

There is a tendency to be susceptible to the cold, easily tired and worse at night. Concentration is difficult although they are much quicker on the uptake than Type 2, yet have difficulty in sticking to the subject in hand.

The consequence of this is that they have some difficulty at school, particularly with mathematics, and are much happier with arts subjects. Often they will start to tell you something but lose the thread of the conversation and go onto another subject. There is a tendency to cry out in the sleep.

They are very attractive children with pale skin and rosy cheeks – the roses being rather localised – with a smooth round face, clear sparkling eyes and faces, and rosy lips.

They tend to have a rather narrow rib cage and brittle nails that can be a problem in that they easily go septic round the cuticle. They are given to headaches and dizziness with coldness of the body. Their headaches often come at weekends and holidays.

Styes are a common occurrence, or yellow discharge from the eyes which forms crusts while sleeping. They hate strong light, particularly artificial light, sunlight being less troublesome.

Ear problems are common, particularly middle ear infections and abcesses in the ear, the discharge from which smells unpleasant. In these days of antibiotics, however, these pustular discharges are rarely seen, the infection having been treated at an earlier stage.

Hay fever and nose bleeds are also common to this type. If old enough to be questioned they may tell you that their saliva tastes either sweet, metallic or bloody.

There is frequently ravenous hunger, with an aversion to meat but a craving for sweet, salt or acid food. Cow's milk does not suit them and will cause problems (see chapter on Feeding Troubles). Diarrhoea tends to come on at night or in the early morning and is worse when cold.

They are susceptible to coughs which are deep, hoarse, worse at night and exhausting. There are long bouts of coughing that come on after being in the cold. The chest seems to suffer whenever they have had a head cold, which always seems to go to the chest.

The child will often wet the bed soon after going to sleep

and tends to pass more urine than other children.

Ankle joints are weak and easily sprained, and the wrist joints are also weak. The hands tend to droop as though the wrists are not strong enough.

There is a tendency to swollen glands, which may be associated with eczema, while Herpes (cold sores) and Urticaria (nettle rash) are other common skin problems in this type.

TYPE 4 (Hydrogenoid)

This child feels the cold and likes to be warm and snug. All symptoms are worse during the day and worse in damp weather. Damp conditions make everything worse. This child will always seem much healthier for a while after having had a cold.

Temperamentally the child is rather irritable and easily gets cross. Rather absent minded and slow in conversation, it will remember events that happened a while ago, but not what you told it yesterday. There is a tendency to be suspicious, especially of new acquaintances, in fact almost taciturn, and the child can be jealous, quarrelsome and selfish.

Sometimes if the circumstances are unfavourable, this type of child can progress to being secretive, telling lies, mischief making and even showing cruelty. An example of this is the child who steals when there are no psychological or unhappy circumstances to account for it.

The complexion is pale and muddy with pale lips and a bluish tinge to the face and nose. Finger nails are thick and ridged. Warts are common and may even appear around the anus or genitals.

Headaches are at the top of the head and are much worse when lying down. They seem to be better for moving about or going for a walk.

Rich foods do not agree with them and they do better on

plain foods. Meat is liked, as are rich foods, but vegetarian foods are much better for them. Shellfish generally causes problems for this type, so be aware that any skin problems may be caused by an allergy to it.

Colic can be troublesome. The colic is relieved by bending double and is better for pressure or lying on the abdomen. As babies, they want to be rocked and carried about.

The diarrhoea of this type is explosive and burning, and comes gushing out. The babies have a tendency to soreness around the anus and appalling nappy rash.

Coughs are worse in the autumn and winter, although after much coughing very little mucous is brought up. Breathing can be depressed and there is a tendency to turn blue. This type is usually a mouth breather too, which will often set them off into a coughing bout. Asthma attacks are common.

A predisposition to urinary infections belongs to this type. Often pain is experienced when passing urine and they will cry and scream, even when there is no infection present.

Skin complaints include acne, barbers' rash, all kinds of pustular eruptions, psoriasis, ringworm, warts, and dry scaly patches. The whole body can even become scaly.

2
Common Illnesses of Children

BED WETTING

I will not dwell here on the mechanical ways of helping this problem, as they have no doubt already been tried. Mothers are well aware that the emotions play a part in this problem. Changes at school and at home, and feelings of insecurity must always be borne in mind. Less often thought of are conditions like worms, a slight infection of the bladder, allergies or changes in temperature. Very often a child will lose the bedcovers in the night, become cold and wet the bed, pull up the covers and carry on sleeping, nobody being any the wiser. It is worth making sure that warm nightwear is worn before trying anything else.

Tension and excitement can also be a cause, and here again tension may not be noticeable, so it is worth making observing the child closely for underlying causes. Often little things that one would never suspect can worry a child, such things as a minor misdemeanour or fear because they have overheard adults' conversations and misinterpreted their meaning. A lazy sphincter at the neck of the bladder may also be at the root of the problem and this will improve as the child matures just as long as the bedwetting is not encouraged to escalate into a psychological problem by much being made of it. Lastly, acidity of the urine will irritate the bladder and cause frequency.

REMEDIES

ARGENT. NIT.

Child craves sweets and salt – causing acidity of the urine.
Likes cool air.
Fears heights.
Passes urine while sleeping.
This child tends to get very anxious about small things.

BELLADONNA

Child stubborn, selfwilled and nervous.
Dribbles during sleep.
Passes urine during the day in large quantities while standing up.
Worse after midnight.
Bladder irritated with burning feeling in urethra.
Child sleeps on stomach or on its side with the head bent back or with arms over the head.

CALCIUM. CARB.

Copious urine with irritable bladder.
Plump chilly children.
Usually rather sensitive and quiet.

CAUSTICUM

Passes urine shortly after falling asleep.
Poor sphincter control due to weakness.
Passes urine while coughing.
Worse from cold weather.

CINA

Dislikes being looked at. Dislikes being touched but likes to be carried.
Grinds teeth in sleep.
Always picking the nose.
Bad tempered and dissatisfied with everything, even things they like or want.

EQUISETUM

Dreams of passing urine.
Pain in bladder is dull with a full feeling – no better for urinating.
Constant desire to urinate.
Sudden onset.

LYCOPODIUM

Passes large quantities of urine while sleeping.
Frequency during the day.
Will cry out when passing urine.
Urine irritates the skin causing redness.

NAT. MUR.

Passes urine involuntarily while walking or coughing.
Craves salty foods or tasty foods.
Cannot pass urine easily in front of other people.
Becomes upset if mother is sympathetic.

PHOSPHORIC ACID

Bed absolutely flooded.
Comes shortly after falling asleep.
Child is usually a delicate type.
Bladder weak.

PHOSPHOROUS

Copious colourless urine.
Child usually slim.
Craves salty foods and ice cream.
Fears ghosts, thunder, the dark and being alone.
Child very affectionate and bright.

PULSATILLA

Child sensitive and weepy – loves sympathy.
Urine offensive in smell.
Sleeps with the arm above the head or on the abdomen.
Tends to dribble when walking or squatting down.

SULPHUR

Running water makes the child want to urinate.
Sudden need to urinate – cannot hold on.
Passes urine whilst dreaming about it.
Copious colourless urine.

THUJA

Frequency of urine with pain.
Sudden desire, cannot wait.
Frequency during the night – always getting up.
Urine smells very strong.

The above remedies are also all useful when there is a urinary infection and the symptoms are a good fit.

COLDS

Some children are prone to catching colds far too frequently, especially when they start school. Children mix together these days at a much earlier age than they used to do. There are social advantages to consider, and the problem is mainly caused by the fact that the immune system is still not mature enough to cope with the onslaught of a vast variety of changing bugs.

The child who is always catching cold belongs to Type 3 and so treatment should start with one dose only of Tuberculinum (1M potency), which may be repeated after an interval of 6 months.

Plenty of fresh air, good food and exercise are desirable, coupled with periodic courses of multivitamin supplements with Zinc. There are a number of good liquid vitamin supplements on the market for children, but Zinc is important and should always be given to these children in addition.

The colds may be treated with the most suitable remedy, but it may be necessary to re-prescribe after a day or two as the symptom picture may change.

REMEDIES

ACONITE

Use immediately symptoms commence.
Chilly, feverish, and thirsty.
Nose running with hot thin discharge.
Nose feels dry and stuffy with sneezing.
Symptoms brought on by exposure to cold.

ALLIUM CEPA

Discharge profuse and watery.
Nose and eyes smarting.
Discharge stops in the open air but starts again on entering warm atmosphere.
Much sneezing.
Top lip is sore.

AMMON. CARB.

Nose blocked at night with much burning coryza.
Cannot breathe through nose.
The end of the nose is red and swollen.
Nose may bleed after eating or washing the face.

ARSEN. ALB.

Wants small drinks and often.
Nose feels stopped up.
No better for sneezing. The nose still feels blocked.
Thin watery discharge which burns the lips.

BRYONIA

Thirsty for long drinks.
Aching in the forehead.
Nose swollen.
Skin round the nose feels tight and dry.

GELSEMIUM

Sluggish, sleepy and dizzy feeling.
Feverish and wants to be warm.
Nose feels very dry and hot inside.
Cold is more catarrhal.

This type of child catches cold in damp muggy weather and every change in the weather.

HEPAR SULPH.

Much catarrh throughout the whole respiratory tract.
Sneezing on going into a cooler atmosphere.
Discharge is yellowish and offensive.
Hoarseness and cough.
Ear troubles usually start or follow a cold.

KALI BICH.

Green or yellow catarrh, thick and stringy, or tough and jellylike.
Violent sneezing with feeling of obstruction in the nose.
The inside of the nose is raw.
Sinusitis may be an added complication.

NAT. MUR.

Discharge is like egg white.
Nose pouring.
Violent sneezing.
Loss of smell and taste.

NUX VOMICA

Oversensitive and irritable.
Nose stopped up at night but runs freely during the day.
Feels cold and cannot get warm.
Fluent discharge which dries up in cool air or outside.
Throat feels rough and scratched.

PULSATILLA

Thick yellowish, bland discharge.

Nose stopped at night but starts to run in the morning. The lips are chapped – feels they must be moistened with the tongue.

No thirst and better in the open air.

COLIC

Here we have a thorny problem indeed, and one which causes great distress to mother and baby. The baby in this case is showing Type 4 constitution symptoms, and before any other treatment is attempted, one does of Medorrhinum 30 potency should be administered. In many cases this will be sufficient, so it is as well to wait for a few days before listing the symptoms, as the baby may change.

Usually bottle fed babies are the sufferers, but colic is certainly not unknown in breast fed babies. Air swallowing is the most common cause, but also the digestive process is at fault. This is basically because the digestive system of the infant is immature and an accumulation of gases from undigested food builds up in the intestine, causing distension and pain. Soothers, which are frowned upon these days, are of great help if the baby will take one, as the constant sucking stimulates the digestive system wonderfully. Provided they are properly sterilised they are perfectly safe. It is never the friend or mother-in-law who criticises the dummy who is having to comfort the screaming infant.

An allergy to cows' milk however should never be overlooked, so the remedies in the chapter on Feeding Problems may be of help, as some babies absolutely refuse point blank to take soya milk. Since soya milk tastes remarkably like emulsion paint one must admit they have a point.

REMEDIES

COLOCYNTH.

Griping pain around navel.
Doubles up with pain.
Relieved by pressure.
An occasional dose of Nux. Vomica will enhance the action of this remedy.

CHAMOMILLA

Pain is unbearable.
Needs to be constantly carried and patted.
Worse at night.
Child screams relentlessly and flails with arms with pure anger.

DIOSCOREA

Worse lying down.
Worse bending forward.
Throws head back and arches the back.
Much rumbling of the abdomen with wind.

MAG .PHOSPH.

Better for pressure.
Better for warm applications.
Abdomen bloated.
Better for passing wind.
Violent hiccough.
This remedy is a good one to combine with another when the indicated remedy does not work well.

STANNUM

Cramp round the navel, relieved by firm pressure.

VERATRUM ALB.

Abdomen swollen.
Very sensitive to pressure.
Cold sweat on forehead.
Cold feet.
Likes cold water but vomits it back.

CONSTIPATION

Two of the most common causes of constipation in infants are cows' milk and wheat intolerence. Breast fed infants rarely suffer from this complaint. If the constipation is persistent it is not a bad idea to try changing the diet, using rice based foods instead of wheat, and boiled milk with vitamin drops as a supplement, or soya if the baby will take it. Raw (not refined) sugar or honey added to the feeds may help.

Constipation can also ensue if the child has a sore, cracked anus and has put off going to the toilet because of the discomfort. Plenty of exercise, fluids and fruit juices are desirable with a little reminder now and again.

Potty training too early can be another reason, and it is better to wait until the child is old enough to have conscious control over its motions. Most children are ready at two years of age but two and a half can be quite normal, particularly in boys. Usually at these ages training can be accomplished in anything from a few days to two to three weeks without tension.

When a child with no conscious control is required to perform and be 'good' and cannot comply, it can become anxious, causing the anal sphincter to be tight, causing constipation. The mother becomes bothered about it and subconsciously so does the child, because it is not able to be 'good'. One can imagine the problems that can ensue from this scenario.

REMEDIES

ALUMINIUM

No desire for stool.
Stools like sheep dung.
Due to inactive rectum.
No desire to go to stool.

BRYONIA

All mucous membranes are dry – even the lips.
Desires lots of drinks.
Stools large, very dry and dark coloured.
Child cries when passing stool.
No desire to have bowel opened.

CALC. CARB.

Stool large, hard and very pale. Second stool much softer.
Suppositories are often necessary to help open the bowel.
Child may be very partial to eggs.

CAUSTICUM

Persistant constipation.
Stools thin like pencils and covered with mucous.
Finds stool easier to pass standing up.
Child's face becomes red with the effort.

LYCOPODIUM

Stools small hard and difficult to pass.

Opening the bowel is painful and causes great distress.
The tummy may be bloated with much wind.
Child hungry but is soon full.

NUX. VOMICA

Child keeps wanting to open the bowel, but only a small
amount comes.
Child may suffer from indigestion and piles.

CHEST COMPLAINTS

Most coughs come as a result of having a cold or sore throat,
but some colds can start with one. If the child is in generally
good health a proprietary cough mixture suitable for
children will usually be sufficient to deal with the problem.
However there are children who are susceptible to
repeated coughs and their chest is obviously their weakest
spot.

Here we have the Type 3 constitution prominent, so one
dose of Tuberculinum 1M potency should be administered.

A word of warning here. If a child has or has had eczema,
do not give any remedy in a high potency, as a skin
aggravation may ensue which you would be unable to deal
with by yourself.

After giving Tuberculinum 1M wait a few days before any
further treatment. If the problem recurs you will find that
the symptoms have been modified. As usual it will then be
necessary to treat the new symptom picture as it appears.

Allergies must be considered in these children. It is very
difficult to tell the difference between an infection and an
allergy and children have been known to have course after
course of antibiotics for these persistent coughs with no

long term benefit. Even more confusing, the allergic cough is often better for a week or two after a course of antibiotics, but comes back very quickly. Become suspicious if the recurring cough is always of the same type. The allergic cough is usually of the dry tickling or wheezing variety but can become catarrhal.

Allergy to house dust and dairy products often produce catarrhal symptoms which, coupled with the other symptoms, will further confuse the issue.

Acute bronchitis is still fairly common in children, but chronic bronchitis is not such a common complaint since the advent of sulphonomides and antibiotics, and the Clean Air Act. Asthmatic coughs however are all too common, and a source of great distress to parents and children alike. The asthmatic constitution falls into the combination of Types 1, 2, and 3, which is why it is so difficult to treat. All cases of asthma have an allergic background coupled with a nervous involvement. They always go together.

Apart from the general treatment, it is very important that the parents do not become over anxious or show undue anxiety when dealing with the child. The child in these circumstances is already anxious because of the difficulty in breathing, and it certainly doesn't want to have to start worrying about how the parent feels. Parents of asthmatic children cannot bear to see them suffer, and it is all too easy to become overprotective. Overprotective attitudes will reinforce the idea in the child that something is badly wrong. A calm, matter of fact attitude will go a long way to reassuring the child that all will be well, as it usually is.

For asthmatic children start treatment with one dose of Thuja 200, followed a week later by one dose of Tuburculin 200. This initial treatment will make a good start in modifying the constitution.

Should there be any further attacks, treat the symptoms as they arise as you would during any other attack. Do not give the aforementioned remedies during an attack, wait a day or two until things have settled down.

It is very important to deal with the allergic problems, as foods can be part of the trouble, particularly milk, wheat, fish and oranges, along with house dust, housedust mite, animal hairs, grasses and pollens.

REMEDIES

ACONITE

Shortness of breath with dry burning throat.
Headache.
Thirsty with flushed face.
Restlessness and anxiety.
Worse at night from cold air.
Wakes up with a smothered feeling.

ANTIMONIUM TARTRATE

Weak, sweating, sleepy and distressed.
Chest sounds full of mucus, but coughs none up.
Wants cold drinks.
Chest rattling with mucus.

ARSEN. ALB.

Child very anxious and unable to breathe properly.
Worse after midnight.
Very restless.
Wants frequent drinks but in small amounts.
Cough dry, teasing, and wheezing.

BRYONIA

Cough hard and dry.
Worse in the daytime.

Worse from eating, drinking, or movement.
Wants to sit up to cough.
Holds chest and head.
Worse going from cool to warm atmosphere.
Wants long cold drinks.
Very irritable.

BELLADONNA

Cough dry with burning and tickling in the larynx.
Spasmodic cough.
Child may cry out when starting to cough.
May cough until sick with the spasms.
Worse at night in bed.
Face flushed with headache.

CAUSTICUM

Trachea raw and sore.
Relieved by drinking cold water.
Cough dry with hardly any expectoration.
Loses a little urine when coughing.

DROSERA

Spasmodic, irritating dry cough.
Vomiting and retching.
Spasms of coughing come close together.
Worse evening and night.
Tickling wakens child up into a coughing bout.
Holds sides of chest when coughing.
Phlegm yellow.

HEPAR SULPH.

Loose cough with hoarseness.
Better in a warm damp atmosphere.

Wants to sit up.
Bends head backwards.
Appears suffocated.
Worse after midnight and in the early hours.

IPECACUANHA

Persistent, violent cough.
Wheezing.
Air passages full of mucus.
Child coughs and goes rigid.
Goes blue in the face or pale.
Relieved by vomiting phlegm.
Feels sick even after vomiting.

KALI BICH.

Ringing cough.
Worse early hours.
Yellow sticky phlegm.
Better for warmth.
Worse after eating, drinking, or cold air.

KALI CARB.

Cough dry and hacking.
Worse around three a.m.
Phlegm coughed up in small lumps.
Child leans forward with head on knees.

LYCOPODIUM

Dry cough with restlessness.
Cough has hollow sound.
Chest sounds full of mucus.
Child angry and wants to be left alone.
Worse approximately from 4 p.m. to 8 p.m.

NUX VOMICA

Dry, teasing, exhausting cough.
Child angry and easily upset.
Soreness in chest.
Mentally very sensitive.
Worse in the morning and after eating or drinking.

PULSATILLA

Cough dry in the evening but loose in the morning.
Expectoration easy to raise.
Worse coming into a warm atmosphere.
Thick yellow or green phlegm.
Worse in a warm room or lying down.
Better in the fresh air, and sitting up.
Cold, weepy, wants comfort and sympathy.

SULPHUR

A great desire for air.
Chest feels heavy.
Breathing difficult.
Dry cough at night.
Productive cough during the day, with yellow phlegm.
Worse lying on back.
Worse breathing deeply.
Better for sitting up.

DIARRHOEA

Diarrhoea is quite common in small children and may not always be due to a tummy bug, particularly when teething. Certain foods upset some children as they are temporarily unable to digest them, or there may be a malfunction in calcium absorption.

Families with animals should be very careful about worms in household pets, and care must be taken to worm pets regularly, as it is all too easy for a child to pick up this infestation.

Information about digestive upsets and intolerance of milk or wheat will be found in the appropriate chapters in this book. Consider these, as these problems can promote diarrhoea of all kinds.

REMEDIES

ARGENT. NIT.

Caused by too much sugar.
Great desire for sweets.
Easily frightened.
Stools green and mucusy, like chopped spinach.

ARSEN. ALB.

Very useful when due to a tummy bug.
Watery, brown, foul stools.
Diarrhoea with burning and sore anus.
Child restless and thirsty for small drinks.
Exhaustion.
Griping pains in abdomen.

BELLADONNA

Useful when teething.
Stools green and watery with white lumps.
Fever with hot head.
Irritability and much complaining.

CALC. CARB.

Useful in teething troubles.
Stools white or pale and bad smelling.
Head hot and sweating.
Feet cold.
Large abdomen.
Stools may be hard but become soft or even liquid after the first motion.

CALC. PHOS.

Useful when teething.
Stools come bubbling out.
Hot slimy stools.
Vomiting with diarrhoea.
Babies want to be fed all the time.
Cold hands and feet.
Fruits disagree with them.

CHAMOMILLA

Stools green or yellow, often alternating.
One cheek hot and red, one pale and cold.
Very bad tempered – nothing will pacify them.
Stools watery and smelly, rather like scrambled egg in appearance, and flecked with green.

DULCAMARA

Stools full of mucus with much pain before passing.
Stools watery green or yellow without control.
Vomiting.
No appetite.
Sleepy and wants to lie down.
Worse for cold weather or weather changing from hot to cold.

MAG. CARB.

Stools green and frothy, with white greasy lumps.
Milk disagrees.
Stools smell sour.
Useful in teething, and combines well with other
remedies.

PODOPHYLLUM

Useful for teething or tummy bugs.
Stool watery green and gushing with mucus lumps.
Worse early morning.
Stools painless but with much wind.
Rolls head from side to side.
Every kind of diarrhoea imaginable is covered by this
remedy, and is the most popular in infants.

EAR ACHE AND OTITIS MEDIA
(Catarrhal and pustular)

As you will see from the chapter on constitutional types,
the child with persistent ear problems falls basically into
the Type 3 constitution.

The first time your child suffers from this painful
complaint it will no doubt need a course of antibiotics as an
emergency treatment. Once this has been dealt with it is
necessary to try to alter the child's constitution.

One dose of Tubeculin 1M potency should be sufficient
to get things on the right road. This should be followed by
one dose of Sulphur 30 two weeks later. It is more than
likely that this treatment will be all that is needed, although
there are stubborn cases which will need further medication.

Should this be the case, symptoms must be treated as they arise, with the remedy that best fits the picture. If the constitution has been somewhat modified and the problem still exists in a milder form, a repetition after six months of the Tuberculin and Sulphur regime is advisable.

REMEDIES

ACONITE

Caused by exposure to cold or sudden changes in temperature.
Ear hot, painful, swollen and throbbing with cutting pain.
Worse at night.
Short acting remedy – suits sudden earache.
Often needs to be followed by another remedy or used in conjunction with one.

BELLADONNA

Face flushed.
Head hot.
Pain comes and goes suddenly.
Worse moving about.
Worse when touched.
Pains deep and going into the throat.
Better from warmth.

CAPSICUM

Swelling and pain behind the ears, going into the mastoid bone.
Cannot bear to have it touched.
Feels chilly with headache.
Pus in the middle ear.

CHAMOMILLA

Child screaming and furious, will often strike out.
Cheeks red.
Pain comes in waves.
Restless and fretting.

FERRUM PHOSPH

Ear dark red.
Pusey discharge.
Eardrum red and bulging.
This remedy is best administered immediately the pain starts.
Use together with best indicated remedy.

HEPAR SULPH.

Throbbing and deafness.
Cannot bear ear to be touched.
Better by hot applications.
Needs to have the body warm.
The slightest draught or cold air will aggravate.
Invariably there is pus involved.

KALI MUR.

Inflammation involves the back of the nose and eustachian tubes.
Swollen glands in the neck.
Noises in the ear.
Sickness.
Often associated with tonsillitis.

LACHESIS

Worse at night.

Worse on left side, but may progress to the right.
Hard wax in the ear.
Better for warmth.
Usually the throat is sore and worse when swallowing.

MERC. SOL.

Thin burning discharge.
Roaring in the ears.
Pain in the face and teeth.
Parotid glands swollen.
Recurring deafness and tonsil problems.
Pain shooting and tearing.

MAG. PHOS.

Relieved by hot compresses.
Pains are spasmodic.
Pains are localised.
Worse for cold.
Better for pressure.

PULSATILLA

Suited to gentle sensitive children.
Pus greenish.
Ear swollen, red, and hot.
Itching deep in the ear.
Deafness.
Very suitable for chronic cases.

PLANTAGO

Pain goes from ear to ear.
Noise unbearable.
Often associated with toothache.

The Schuessler tissue salts are good to use from time to time on a long term basis to assist in the treatment of ear problems. A combination of these given for one week in every month for six months will help tremendously, but are rarely enough on their own. The tissue salts are available at most Pharmacies these days and at health food stores. A combination of the following is useful:

> Mag. Phos. 6
> Ferrum Phos. 6
> Calc. Phos. 6
> Silica 6

All four should be taken together 3 times daily.

ECZEMA

The types and causes of eczema are varied indeed, but can be loosely categorised into two main groups in the constitutions.

Type 1 – This inheritance causes papular eczema. This means that the eczema starts as small raised spots which are sometimes just under the surface of the skin. Scratching causes the skin to break down and become infected. The eczema will then weep a serous fluid which is straw coloured and sticky. A herbal eczema ointment is beneficial here as it helps to keep the itching at bay and dry it up.

Type 2 – The eczema of Type 2 is already pustular and will first manifest itself as small pustules. It is very important that the skin be kept as clean as possible to stop the infection from spreading.

Type 3 – Here the skin is dry and flaky, sometimes so much so that the child's bed is full of dry scales in the morning. The skin is thickened and the dead skin flakes continually, even the parts of the body that are unaffected by the eczema are dry.

So we see that the child has the same constitution as the asthmatic child, and eczema that is suppressed will progress to asthma in some cases. It is really very important that at the first sign of eczema the best homoeopathic remedy should be applied before the complaint takes a firm hold.

Cortisone creams may seem like the answer, and work like magic the first few times they are used, but this is suppression and eventually they will cease to work. Worse still the child very often becomes allergic to the ointment and the problem gets worse. Cortisone creams also make the skin fragile so that the skin breaks down even more easily.

If a child shows signs of eczema in the first few months of life the culprit is more than likely a cows' milk allergy. Even breast fed infants may have this tendency because the mother herself has a cows' milk allergy. It may be worthwhile the mother giving up cows' milk whilst feeding and provided she eats a good diet this should cause no problem if she takes calcium with Vitamins A & D as a supplement.

As with asthma the child is probably emotionally sensitive so care must be taken to deal with it calmly. Every mother wants her baby to be perfect, and the sight of a blemished skin can cause great anxiety. Not all eczemas itch and often the mother's suffering exceeds that of the child. The solicitude of friends and grandmothers is not much help either, as they can make an already anxious mother feel inadequate – don't let them, it is nobody's fault and will not help to mend the situation.

Allergies play an important part in eczema simply because the inherited constitution is allergic. Egg, wheat, cows' milk, oranges, apples, and other common foods can either cause or exacerbate eczema.

It is worth mentioning here that eggs, oranges and fish

are the outstanding culprits in hives, so if your child suffers from hives after eating these foods there is an allergy there most certainly.

When selecting ointments to help with itching and dryness never use petroleum based products, particularly Vaseline. Try herbal cleansers and eczema soaps. Never use baby oils or scented talcum powders, as these have petroleum products in them unless otherwise labelled.

Read labels carefully and consult your pharmacist or health store if you are looking for herbal salves and cleansers. Wash with soap as little as possible, even eczema soaps. Sponge the affected areas with a saline solution – one teaspoonful of sea salt to one pint of water. A good cleansing and healing solution is:- One teaspoonful of sea salt with a few drops of Mother Tincture of Calendula and Hypericum in one pint of water, preferably purified.

Any chemist who sells homoeopathic remedies will order these for you. An adequate intake of Vitamins A, D, and C, is essential as is the tissue salt Calcium Phosphate, particularly if the child is a poor eater.

REMEDIES

ARSEN. ALB.

Itching and burning and better for warmth.
Skin very dry.
Child and eczema worse for being cold.
Usually a delicate looking child with fine skin.
Site – face, head, and legs.

DULCAMARA

Eczema is moist.
Itching and burning.
Yellow brown crusts.

Thin yellow discharge.
Worse cold and damp.
Site – face, hands, and between the legs.

GRAPHITES

Skin rough and dry with cracks.
Sticky honey coloured discharge.
Burning and itching.
Site – behind the ears, between the fingers and in the bends of the joints, scalp and eyelids.

HEPAR SULPH.

Prickling.
Easily becomes infected.
Very sensitive to the touch.
Discharge yellowish.
Bleeds easily.
Better for being covered up.
Site – head, face and eyelids.

LACHESIS

Left sided eczema or started on the left and spread to the right.
Eruptions bluish or with a mauve cast.
Site – any part of the body but especially the legs.

LYCOPODIUM

Right sided eczema, or starting on the right and spreading to the left.
Worse for warmth.
Discharge yellow which comes after scratching.
Site – face, legs, and between the legs.

MERCURIUS

Worse from the warmth of the bed.
Yellow brown crusts.
Bleeds easily.
Eczema is moist.
Site – face and scalp.

NAT.MUR.

Skin greasy.
Eruptions look beefy red.
Very itchy and raw.
Site – hair line and often the forehead.

I have mentioned the most common sites on the body for each remedy. However if the symptom pattern fits regardless of the site, use the remedy. It is always a good idea to give Berberis Vulgaris 3 times daily for 7 days before giving the chosen remedy, as this helps the kidneys to eliminate some of the toxins in the body and the remedy itself will be more efficient.

FEEDING PROBLEMS

Some children seem to be unable to digest milk satisfactorily, and even mother's milk may cause problems. These babies will often respond to Tuberculin Bovine 200 potency one dose. If this fails it is necessary to observe carefully the kind of vomiting or posseting involved. They will probably at the same time have colic and other bowel disturbances. So when trying to pick the remedy it is as well to check these symptoms against the colic remedies as it will help to pinpoint the right one.

It is very important to check this condition as soon as possible, as the milk proteins left undigested will lead to a milk allergy.

REMEDIES

ARSEN. ALB.

Instant vomiting with diarrhoea.
Thirsty for cold water which causes pain, followed by vomiting.
Diarrhoea worse at night after midnight.
Baby restless irritable and weak.

CALC. CARB.

Milk vomited in sour lumps.
Stools passed with white curds.
Head sweaty with cold feet.
Very hungry and thirsty.
Stool may also be claylike, green and watery.
Angry before stool.
Very similar to a sulphur baby but with more white curds in the stool.

LYCOPODIUM

Always hungry but soon stops feeding.
Wants feeding again after getting wind up.
Stomach distended after feeding.
Pressure aggravates.
Wind rumbling especially on the left side.

MAG. CARB.

Watery burning stools – white or putty coloured.

Acute enteritis.
Chilly yet better in the open air.
Milk disagrees – sour vomiting.
Better for movement.

SEPIA

Cannot take even boiled milk.
Seems much worse when teething.
Generally wakeful but worse around three a.m.
Green painless stools.

SILICA

Delicate child with a poor appetite.
Aversion to mothers' milk.
Vomits immediately after feeding.
Stools watery and smelly or may be constipated.

SULPHUR

The baby is very hungry.
Vomits back the milk undigested.
May be constipated or have green watery, slimy stools.
Worse at night.
Usually wakens at about 5 a.m. with a bowel movement.
Fitful sleep and screaming in the night.
May dislike his bath or being washed.

3
Infectious Diseases

CHICKEN POX

REMEDIES

APIS. MEL.

Skin and eyelids puffy.
Worse for warmth.
Thirstless with very little urine.
Skin itches terribly.

BELLADONNA

Red face and eyes.
Skin very hot.
Headache and fever.
Very little thirst.
Sleepy but cannot drop off.

RHUS TOX

Very restless.
Worse at night – doesn't want to stay in bed.
Coated tongue with a red tip.
Pus in the eyes.
Complains of being stiff.

SULPHUR

Skin itching and burning.
Worse for being washed.
Skin very dry.
Much scratching.
Lips and anus may be red.

JAUNDICE

REMEDIES

ARSEN.ALB.

Restless, anxious and weak.
Better for being warm.
Skin and whites of the eyes yellow.
Pain in the liver.
Stools white and smelly.
Urine dark yellow or brown.
Thirsty for small quantities.

BRYONIA

Skin and eyes yellow.
Pain in liver, better when resting.
Thirst for long drinks frequently.
Constipation with no desire to move bowels, or soft loose stools.
Headache with faintness, worse for movement.
Nausea.
Bitter taste in mouth, with cracked dry lips.
Urine yellow or brown.

CHELIDONIUM

Pain under right shoulder blade.
Clay coloured stools.
Skin and eyes yellow.
Nausea and vomiting, with a bitter taste.
Hands very cold.
Tongue coated yellow.
Chilly with fever.
Desire for sour tasting foods.

PODOPHYLLUM

Stools green and offensive if very loose.
Constipation with clay coloured stools.
Urine dark.
Skin and eyes yellow.
Tongue very dirty.
Rolls the head from side to side.

MEASLES

REMEDIES

APIS

Child not thirsty.
Difficult breathing.
Cannot do with being in a warm room.
Throat swollen and skin puffy.
Passes very little urine.
Sore chest with cough.
The rash does not come out properly.

ARSEN. ALB.

Itching and burning of the skin.
Worse after midnight.
Wants lots of small drinks often.
Anxious and restless.
Very weak.
There may be diarrhoea.

BELLADONNA

Difficulty in swallowing.
Convulsions when the rash appears.
High temperature.
Red eyes and red face.
Throbbing head.

GELSEMIUM

Feverish and chilly.
Running nose.
Croupy cough.
Skin cold and itching, the spots are very red.
Headache with red face.
Thirstless.

PULSATILLA

Eyes discharging and sticky.
Spots dark red.
Thick yellow mucus from nose.
Dry cough during the night, but loose in the daytime.
Must sit up to cough.
Thirstless.
Lips very dry, wants to moisten them.

MUMPS

REMEDIES

ARSEN. ALB.

Useful in an arsen. alb. type of child.
Child feels cold.
Warm compresses give relief.

BELLADONNA

Swelling of the right parotid gland.
Flushed face.
High temperature.
Child may be confused.

LACHESIS

Left sided.
Glands very sensitive to touch.
Difficulty swallowing – even the saliva.
Face red and swollen.
Worse at night and on awakening in the morning.

LYCOPODIUM

Begins on the right side, and may progress to the left.
Throat inflamed.
Better for warm drinks.

MERCURIUS SOLUBILIS

Pale swelling of the gland.
Temperature not so high.
There is much saliva which smells bad.

Swellings better for cold compresses.
Swellings very hard and testes may be swollen in small boys.

PULSATILLA

Chilly and thirstless.
Ear may be infected.
Mouth dry.
Worse in the evening or lying down.
Testes may be swollen or the breasts in the case of girls.

RHUS. TOX.

Glands very angry and red.
Worse left side.
Difficulty in opening the mouth.
Very restless and worse from draughts.
Neuralgia of the face.

SPASMODIC CROUP

The epiglottis is the small flap of cartilage at the top of the wind pipe, which normally opens and closes when we breath. For some unknown reason it can go into a spasm, stopping the air from leaving the lungs. It is an alarming experience for both mother and child, particularly as the mother can mistake it for a convulsion (fit).

It is often confused with croup or asthma. Normally the croupous cough is associated with an infection such as laryngitis, and is a crowing cough, whereas the wheezings of asthma are lower down in the chest, or under the breast bone.

Spasmodic croup occurs mainly in the first year of life,

and the causes are debatable. It is thought that it may be an irritation of the laryngeal nerve, an allergic response, enlarged lymph glands, or purely a nervous complaint, and one has to say that it does seem to occur in infants of a sensitive disposition, particularly if they have not been very well.

It is absolutely essential that the mother does not appear anxious, which is not easy as the first attack happens very suddenly, leaving mother and child somewhat shaken. The first and most important thing is to get the child to breathe. This can be done by pouring a jug or two of cold water over the back or chest, or putting the child first in cold water and then in warm alternately.

Tickling is another good method, either in the ribs or anywhere that you know the child to be ticklish. Tickling is very good as the whole business ends in fun, which diffuses the anxiety.

The constitution is usually predominantly Type 1 overlaid with 3 and 4. Sulphur is a remedy that covers all three types well, so give a dose of Sulphur 30 daily for three days to start with. If there is a recurrence, choose the most suitable remedy as the spasms will always be the same, and administer one dose of the 30th potency if an attack occurs again.

If there is an improvement but not a complete cure, administer Psorinum 30, one dose. Should the symptoms change, reassess the prescription. Happily this condition is something that children seem to grow out of, but there is no consolation to the child.

In slightly older children the spasms often occur if they have been chastised, or when things have not been going their way, so it is important to be calm. Sometimes it is possible that the onset of these episodes comes on a few weeks after an immunisation. If the connection between these events is obvious, start the whole treatment with a dose of Thuja 30. This will antidote the side effects of the vaccine, and may in fact be all that is required.

Once again it is very important to stress that the mother shows no anxiety, or discusses it in front of relatives and friends. The knack is to be firm, competent and apparently unhurried when dealing with this crisis.

SYMPTOMS   The child stops breathing and crows as it tries to breath. Breathing out is almost impossible, and the child tries to breathe in without success.

The head is thrown back with the hands and toes flexed. The face can go red or blue and the eyes staring.

REMEDIES

CHLORINE

Inhalation easy with crowing.
Exhalation impossible.
Lungs become distended.
Face red.
Partial coma followed by relaxation which ends the episode.

LACHESIS

Spasms occur during sleep or on awakening.
Wakes up gasping for breath.
This child dislikes clothing that fits closely up to the neck at any time.

PHYTOLACCA

Muscles of the eyes are affected, and the eyes seem to work independently.
The thumbs are pressed into the palms of the hands.
Toes are flexed.
Face distorted.

Attacks are frequent.

SPONGIA

Whistles on trying to breathe in.
Starts up from a sleep and has an attack.
Head bent backwards when trying to breathe.

TONSILS AND ADENOIDS

Tonsillitis is a persistent and debilitating complaint, which may or may not involve the adenoids. These glands have an important function, as they are the first line of defence against infections, which is why the fashion for removing them has largely died out. Tonsils swell and become inflamed because they are dealing with infections, keeping invading germs localised in the body. There are people of a certain constitution whose tonsils have to work harder and are not as efficient, and these are the individuals who suffer so much with tonsillitis.

The constitution here is Type 3 with overtones of Types 1 and 2. As recommended in ear troubles start the treatment with a dose of Tuberculinum 1m potency, followed two weeks later by Sulphur 30 one dose. Repeat after six months if necessary. Treat every new attack with the best indicated remedy.

REMEDIES

ACONITE

Feverish with sore throat especially after being chilled.
Throat red, dry, and feels tight.

Nose may be dry and blocked.
Swallowing painful.
Throat burning and prickling.
Child may seem anxious.

APIS

Tonsils swollen and puffed up. Burning and stinging
when swallowing.
Better for cold drinks and ice cream.
Child not thirsty.

BARYTA CARB.

Septic tonsils every time the child gets a cold. Glands
under the jaw swollen.
Worse on the right side.
Smarting in the throat when swallowing the saliva.
Feels as though something is stuck in the throat.

BELLADONNA

Tonsils bright red.
Worse on the right side.
Face flushed with eyes very bright.
Throat tight and dry, and painful when swallowing
liquids.
No thirst.
Feels must cough something up.
Tonsils may be ulcerated.
Bad breath and much saliva.

HEPAR SULPH.

Feels there is a splinter in the throat.
Pain in the ear and lower jaw.
Cold air and draughts aggravate.

Child feels chilly.
Oversensitive to pain, can't bear to be examined.
Tonsils have septic yellow spots.

KALI MUR.

Difficult breathing.
Much catarrh extending into the ears.
Grey patches on the tonsils.
Glands of the neck enlarged.
Tongue heavily coated grey towards the back.

LACHESIS

Tonsils are purple or plum red.
Tightness round the throat aggravates, can't bear collars.
Worse left side, and progresses to the right side.
Wants to swallow continually.
Throat feels swollen inside.
Pain extends from throat to the ear.
Worse for warm drinks.

MERC. SOL.

More useful for septic tonsils with ulceration.
Very thirsty.
Pain swallowing saliva.
Throat raw and burning.
Tongue is puffy, flabby and heavily coated.
The pattern of the teeth may be seen round the edges of
the tongue.

PHYTOLACCA

Worse on the right side.
Pain extends into the ears.
Tonsils very swollen.

Worse in damp weather.
Worse when moving about.
Better when warm and resting.
Throat dry and dark red.
Throat feels too small and rough inside.

SILICA

Pricking pain as if being stabbed.
May feel as though there is a hair on the tongue.
Abcesses.
Child usually delicate and pale.
A useful remedy for chronic cases.

Here again the tissue salts as recommended in ear troubles can be very useful given in the same way. If completely satisfactory results have not been obtained in six months, give one dose of Lueticum 200 followed by one dose of Sulphur 30 two weeks later.

WHOOPING COUGH

REMEDIES

ANTIMONIUM TARTRATE

Rattling of mucus.
Coughing ends in vomiting.
Must sit up – appears to be suffocating.
Face covered in cold sweat.
Tongue thickly coated white.
Very sleepy.
Wants cold drinks often.

BELLADONNA

Cough hard, dry and barking.
Feverish with flushed face.
Appears frightened and clutches the throat.
Whoops with gagging.

CARBO. VEGETALIS

Face red.
Gagging and vomiting with retching.
Wants air with windows open.
Wants to be fanned.
Very exhausted.

CUPRUM METALLICUM

Cough violent.
Prostration and convulsions.
Child black and blue with rigidity.
Cramps in the extremities.

DROSERA

Barking cough, deep and hoarse.
Worse after midnight.
Can't get the breath in a coughing spasm.
The abdomen is sucked inwards in a coughing spasm.
Vomiting of food.

IPECACUANHA

Cough with nausea and vomiting.
Coughing bouts very close together.
There is much sticky mucus.
Child goes stiff and becomes pale or blue.

4
Constitutional Remedies

IMPROVING GENERAL HEALTH WITH HOMOEOPATHY

Apart from the constitutional Types 1, 2, 3, and 4 which have already been discussed, there are a number of remedies that will be useful in treating your child. The ones that I will be discussing are the ones that I have found most useful in treating youngsters of all ages.

You will see that I have dwelt mainly on the mentalities, with only some of the physical symptoms to help choose the remedy. When used correctly they can alter the temperament of the child for the better.

If the child is for example a Pulsatilla type now, it does not mean that it always has been and always will be. Very often once the chosen remedy has done its work, you will have uncovered a different type; so observe the changes and re-prescribe if necessary.

Do not however abandon the original remedy too soon. If it works well and holds for some time, but then slips back, repeat the original remedy. Only re-prescribe if there is a definite change to another remedy. You are not going to be able to change the basic character, but to help the mind and body to make adjustments for the better.

When you read homoeopathic texts about miraculous changes being brought about by one dose of the 30 potency, it must be remembered that most of them were written a long time ago, and circumstances have changed.

With babies and toddlers these miracles can still be achieved, but as the child gets older it becomes more difficult as the drugs that we use today and the type of food we eat can influence the way we react to the remedies.

If children are treated right from the start with homoeopathic and herbal remedies they will be healthier both now and in the future.

It must be remembered that until the 1930s most medicines were based on herbs. Now that manufactured synthetic drugs are used our bodies have to deal with them as well as disease.

Synthetic drugs and suppression of symptoms damage the immune system with long term use, consequently making us weaker and unable to fight back when our bodies are attacked by disease.

There are times however, when it is necessary to resort to these methods, and antibiotics and other drugs are necessary. This last statement may not go down well with my profession, but when treating your family yourself, never take risks. It is not always easy to find a homoeopath or herbalist, and certainly not in a hurry.

By using this book however, you will be able to cut down your visits to the doctor by treating your child's constitution between any crises that may occur, and you will need him less and less. There is no reason why you should not give the correct remedy in acute cases along with the doctor's treatment.

The body will only build up a good immunity if it is allowed to fight its own battles. We have come to expect to get better within 48 hours of being taken ill. Sleep, bed rest and convalescence have gone by the board to the detriment of the nation's health. It is unnatural to be ill with the 'flu on Friday and expect to be better by Monday morning. It is asking too much of our bodies, and eventually we will pay the price with chronic disease in later life.

Treating the mentalities with low potencies such as 6 and 30 is a complete waste of time in young people, as the results will be poor. In ascending order start with 200, and repeat later with 1m potency if and when necessary. Even better results will be achieved in even higher potencies, but a visit to a homoeopath is recommended for this.

ARSEN. ALB.

Physically these children look rather delicate, having fine hair, skin, and bone structure. They are pale, but flush easily, with a hot head and cold extremities, particularly when they are tired or over excited. They are very often both.

They catch cold easily, the type of cold that develops into a sore throat and bronchitis. Asthmatic attacks and skin problems are common, and will often alternate with one another. The asthma is dry and wheezing, but towards the end of an attack will come white, frothy sputum.

The skin problems are dry and itchy, and much worse for scratching. Psoriasis and herpes are common in the Arsen. Alb. types.

The digestive system is very unstable; fruits, ice cream and watery foods can give them diarrhoea. They are usually thirsty for lots of small cold drinks, although sometimes they like warm drinks and find them comforting.

Their senses are over sensitive, noticing every smell and remarking on it. Smells can upset them, even making them sick, as can noise and light. Periodic headaches in older children, of the migraine type, coming on regularly at weekly or fortnightly intervals, are common.

Already overconscientious, they cannot do with being overworked at school, or put under pressure, as they can develop tics (compare with Ignatia).

Mentally they are hypersensitive, and are easily frightened. Afraid of being alone and going out alone, they will even get up in the night and go looking for company. Small children particularly want to sleep with someone. They are terribly restless and always on the go, but exhaust themselves with it and want to lie down.

A vivid imagination makes them have nightmares, and matters are made worse as they are afraid of the dark anyway. Fear is a very prominent symptom in these types. They are always afraid that something will go wrong, and the slightest hitch in their plans throws them completely.

They are very fastidious and tidy, getting very upset if things are out of place – even small children can be like this. Everything has to be just so, rooms nice and tidy, arrangements cut and dried, times worked out, in fact everything spot on. With a tendency to be critical, the happy go lucky types drive them mad.

For all the anticipation and anxiety they can become depressed and even suicidal, having burned themselves out with worry and the desire to do everything right.

When they are ill they are hypersensitive to pain, and quite sure that no treatment will do them any good, to the point of refusing to take their medicine. It will be necessary to give this remedy in a high potency such as 1m or higher, as for mental symptoms it works poorly in low potencies in young people.

BARYTA CARB.

The key word for this remedy is – LATE. These children are late to talk, late to walk, late teething, in fact everything is delayed. It is a matter of degree here and can range from being rather slow to outright backwardness, even to being educationally subnormal. Don't be put off using this remedy by the description of it, if the symptoms fit use it.

Do not however use Baryta if you have already given Calc. Carb., so compare the two remedies carefully. No harm will have been done, but no good will be done either.

The weight of these children can be quite normal, but more often there is a tendency to be overweight.

Glandular and tonsil troubles are the bane of their lives. Every cold starts with a sore throat, progressing to swollen and septic tonsils. The neck glands, axillary glands, and often the glands in the groin swell too. A good starving is almost sure to bring on tonsillitis, as they are very susceptible to the cold, being chilly individuals. Their colds are very mucusy, with crusts in the nose and a swollen top lip. The hands and feet feel cold and the feet sweat a cold offensive sweat. They stand badly too and the spine has a tendency to be crooked. This is not easy to spot in small children, but becomes more obvious in older children and teenagers.

A poor appetite is the norm along with a poor digestion and a dislike of cold food. Eating makes them sleepy and they can become very lethargic after a meal. They are thirsty children and make a lot of saliva particularly during sleep.

Prone to skin troubles of the crusty, itchy variety, which normally appear about the head and eyelids and are much worse for being washed.

Headaches come at the front of the head, with heaviness of the eyes which they have a job to keep open. Mentally it is very difficult to keep their attention for more than a few minutes at a time, and this is particularly noticeable when playing with them as there is complete lack of concentration.

Learning at school is well nigh impossible, as they immediately forget what they have just learned, and by next day can hardly remember anything at all. Lessons have to be repeated again and again, so very intensive teaching is required. Learning tires them out, and as they are usually permanently tired anyway, it completely exhausts them.

Shyness is a problem too, as they are excessively shy, particularly of strangers, even to the extent of being afraid of people altogether. Being left alone distresses them even though they are so shy; yet on the other hand they hate being noticed and interference of any kind makes them extremely irritable.

They are prone to having nightmares and distressing dreams, made worse by the fact that they cannot tell you what they were about.

Give this remedy in the 1m potency and repeat at the slightest sign that the benefit is wearing off. Only progress to another remedy when the symptoms change. Intersperse this remedy with an occasional dose of Lueticum 30 or 200.

CALCIUM CARBONATE

The Calc. Carb. personality usually starts life as a plump, well nourished looking baby, with a tendency to diarrhoea with pale stools. Although they appear to be strong looking children to begin with, they are inclined to be overweight and lacking energy, with a tendency to be lazy.

They feel the cold, but quickly become hot on exertion. The head becomes particularly warm, with a tendency to sweat at night and dampen the pillow. Although their feet feel cold during the day, they become hot at night and they must poke them out of the bed to cool down.

There is a dislike of meat and hot food, they much prefer ice cream. Eggs are a popular food for them and there will often be an actual craving for them. If this symptom is there, then the remedy is almost specific. Glandular problems predominate. If they are ill they will invariably have swollen glands in the neck, or under the arms, and will even have swollen glands without suffering from a specific illness.

Mentally the child is of a shy, retiring nature, easily upset, and certainly cannot do with being teased or laughed at. Often they are slow walkers and talkers.

Co-ordination is poor, with a tendency to be clumsy, so games at school cause great distress as they cannot play them very well. Consequently at school they get left out, which since they are already retiring makes them feel like social outcasts. If this situation is not rectified at an early age it is easy to see why psychological problems can develop. There is a tendency to give in easily and they don't persist with anything that seems difficult for them.

Lessons are the same, if there is a subject that they find difficult they will just abandon the whole thing, getting further and further behind and feeling helpless. Even though they tend to cut themselves off for fear of failure, they are not complete loners and like to have somebody around.

They are nervous children and even though seemingly placid are easily frightened, particularly of the dark and like to have a nightlight.

Children like this are a teacher's nightmare, as they are constantly pressurising the child to join in the games, little realising that they are making matters worse.

Certainly there is no reason why they should not be gently encouraged to keep trying because co-ordination does improve with repeated practice, but as long as the child feels sensitive to ridicule not much progress will be made. Individual sports suit them much better than team games, as the onus is not on them not to let the side down.

I must say here that I have come across many children with none of the physical symptoms of this remedy who have had great benefit from it. It is a remedy which will stand repeating well, so I would suggest the 1m potency, as many as three or four doses in a year. As the child gets older it may evolve into another remedy the most likely being Calc. Phos., Sulphur, or Lycopodium, so watch out for this.

CALCIUM PHOSPHATE

There are some similarities in the Calc.Phos. child to the Calc.Carb. child, and very often a Calc.Carb. baby will evolve into a Calc.Phos. toddler.

These children have difficulty in absorbing calcium, so the teeth and bones are of poor quality. They are thin pale children often with an under developed lower jaw, so the chin is rather receded.

Babies are inclined to teething troubles, having a good deal of difficulty bringing them through, and they tend to decay very quickly whether or not they eat sweets (although we all know by now that too many sweets cause the teeth to decay).

Calcium is absorbed in the stomach, and sugar eaten at the same meal as calcium-containing foods inhibits the absorption of calcium. It is important therefore not to feed sweet foods and dairy products at the same time. Wherever possible fructose (fruit sugar) is preferable to cane sugar when sweetening a baby's food.

These children have a tendency to diarrhoea especially when teething – a green spluttering, windy stool. They love cold drinks, fruits and ice cream which can also promote diarrhoea. Some Calc. Phos. children are very partial to ham, bacon, and smoked meats and will often beg the raw bacon rinds or cooked ones for that matter.

Calcium and Vitamin D supplements in the winter, and plenty of sunshine in the summer are beneficial, together with all the calcium tissue salts and silica to promote absorption. Growing pains are common in this type and as they grow older there is a tendency to become spotty.

There are also glandular problems, but less marked than in the Calc. Carb. type. There will be less trouble with the tonsils than with the adenoids, consequently they tend to be mouth breathers.

Mentally they have a poor memory which makes learning difficult. They understand the subject well enough at the time since comprehension is not difficult but soon forget all about it. At any stage in their development they can be fretful, out of sorts, and extremely touchy.

As the child gets older and starts school headaches become a problem, and girls have a tendency to become anaemic.

They can become exasperating when ill as they dwell on their sufferings, and the more they think about their illnesses the worse they feel. Being cross is useless since they are so touchy – distraction is bound to work better. Even though they are a bit neurotic about their ailments there is a marked dislike of interference.

What the Calc. Phos. type really likes most of all is change – always wanting something different but never sticking with it very long.

So here we have another problem child where school is concerned, with their apparent brightness hampered by a poor memory. They really do feel easily upset, weak, and lacking in enthusiasm, but with the right treatment will respond very well.

GRAPHITES

Physically these children are plagued with skin problems, which are very characteristic. There is not the redness as in Sulphur, so always be careful to notice the difference as giving Sulphur to these children will make them worse.

The eruptions ooze a thick, honey-coloured fluid which tends to lift the scabs away from the skin. The skin has cracks, some of which are very deep. The affected parts are behind the ears, on the scalp, in the folds of the knees and the crook of the elbows. The corners of the mouth may crack and the genitals and anus could also be affected. The legs may be covered with eruptions, and not to be overlooked is Psoriasis in the palms of the hands. The eyelashes tend to grow inwards causing conjunctivitis and styes, while older children and teenagers are prone to acute attacks of acne.

These children tend to be overweight and flabby even to the point of obesity. The obesity in teenagers is often coupled with late periods, and possibly a very white vaginal discharge which causes burning and itching. They are often constipated, the stools being large and hard. If they do have diarrhoea it tends to be watery and brown with lumps in it. A mucous discharge from the anus is burning and itching, often accompanied by piles.

Particular symptoms to look for are – always feels cold, feels as though there is a cobweb on the face and stomach pains relieved by food. They dislike sweets, fish, and sometimes meat. Everybody thinks that they must eat too many sweets because they are plump and spotty, so it comes as rather a surprise when they don't like sweet things.

Do not be put off using the remedy if they are not plump, if the skin symptoms agree.

Mentally these children are very much 'down' when they are older, but not so much so when they are small.

Younger children are not shy, and will even laugh if they are chastised. If you take them to other peoples' houses they are inclined to have a root about and go around picking things up and putting them down anywhere. In fact they can be a general nuisance, even looking in cupboards. Undismayed when reprimanded they will blithely carry on and take not a bit of notice.

As they get older there is a tendency for them to think they are badly done by, and that others have all the luck; in fact generally sorry for themselves. Their ill luck however is due to lack of effort on their own part, as they are indecisive, mentally lazy, and can't be bothered. Usually cheerful enough in the morning, they start to go off by the afternoon and as the day progresses become thoroughly weepy and miserable, crying for no reason.

There is a liking for being alone as other people get on their nerves, which is why they appear so impatient and touchy. They come round wonderfully however when consoled.

They have a keen sense of smell and often dislike the smell of flowers, and they are sensitive to music which will bring tears to their eyes.

IGNATIA

Physically Ignatia has some strange symptoms. In sore throats for instance, the pain is better for swallowing something solid, while a pain in the body is relieved by pressure to the affected part or from lying on it. Stomach symptoms are contradictory too. The kind of foods one would expect to soothe an upset stomach are vomited, whilst indigestible foods are digested without any trouble.

There is no thirst in fever where one would expect it, but there is thirstiness when they have been chilled. Coughing bouts get worse for coughing rather than better, so we see that these subjects suffer from contradictory symptoms.

Ignatia children cannot stand smells, especially tobacco smoke, and they are also given to sighing and yawning. Older children can complain of feeling as though they have a lump in the throat, and although the lump feels real to them, it is in fact a symptom of anxiety.

The stomach suffers when this remedy is indicated, and it may be worth considering in sensitive children who are always complaining of tummy ache. Milk and meat do not suit them well and they may in fact like neither. A nervous tummy is the best description I can give here. They like bread, sour flavours and prefer cold food.

Bowel pain and either constipation or diarrhoea can be common complaints. Ignatia can definitely be useful in colitis of nervous children as this complaint is very often of nervous origin.

Mentally: once again, like physical symptoms, Ignatia is full of contradictions.

These children are very bright and forward at school, but they are prone to tics and nervous headaches when under stress, and their fine coordination suffers so that their writing is bad. Therefore they should not be pushed into excelling even more in order to satisfy teachers and parents – they are bright enough already. Such practices can cause facial twitching and difficulty in speaking, and once acquired are very difficult to get rid of. Overwork can cause the child to become 'switched off' so that they cannot do their homework, or work at school either, and the memory becomes poor.

When pushed to overwork they can go to pieces completely, even to the point of sitting for an examination and not being able to write a word. This can completely ruin a child's career, as very often they will drop out of a course never to take it up again. The parents are permanently disappointed in them, which is no help at all and the spend the rest of their lives feeling let down. It is up to the parents to watch out for this at school, as very often teachers are guilty of trying to push a brilliant pupil.

Small children are highly strung and hypersensitive. Noise drives them mad, especially if they are trying to concentrate and they will fly off the handle and cry. Generally they prefer to be alone. They can also become afraid of they know not what, or be afraid of going out, and afraid of making decisions.

The moods are changeable, and change rapidly from being on a high, laughing and cheeky to being down and weepy. In fact their behaviour can be totally irriational, having apparently no logic to it.

Criticism is taken badly, as they are conscientious. It will send them into a fine old rage, followed by complete breakdown into floods of tears.

Headaches usually come after overwork, and the head feels congested especially between the eyebrows – better for pressure and hot applications.

This remedy is always associated in peoples' minds, and homoeopathic literature, with hysterical females, but there are plenty of boys who will benefit from Ignatia so it should never be overlooked.

Girls who are Nat. Mur. subjects can fall in love easily with some impossible boy, but Ignatia is not as deep as Nat. Mur. They do grieve however from their broken hearts, and Ignatia is an outstanding remedy for grief. The grieving of Nat. Mur. is more of a sad, reclusive grief while Ignatia is a much noisier affair, and sooner over.

Ignatia can be a useful remedy in menstrual problems in young girls when the personality symptoms agree.

LYCOPODIUM

Physically these children are thin, and the skin a little on the sallow side, with rounded tummies which become more noticeable as they grow older. They are not exactly shy, but a little diffident, even though they appear to have quite a bit of confidence in themselves.

The appetite appears good as they are always eager for

food, but they are soon full and will leave half of it, although not all are like this all the time.

Digestive upsets plague the Lycopodium type. They have quite a lot of wind with gurgling, distention, burping, and passing of wind. The digestive process is sluggish. Warm food and drinks are liked, and they are not keen on cold foods. There is a definite liking or even a craving for sweet foods, and shellfish are well liked although they will probably make them sick. If they waken in the night they will more than likely ask for food.

The ailments in the Lycopodium type start on the right side of the body and progress to the left, and all their symptoms are worse in the late afternoon and early evening – approximately 4p.m. to 8p.m.

Small children will sometimes cry out before passing urine, this is a peculiar symptom of Lycopodium. There may be no urinary infection but the urine may be very strong smelling and there may be a red sediment in the nappy. There is a strong desire to pass urine, but when they get on the potty they cannot start easily, the feeling seems to go off as soon as they sit down. This applies to older children too.

Sometimes there is constipation because the anus is tightly closed, so when they have passed a hard stool the mucous membrane will protrude slightly. The stool is hard to start with but is followed by a soft stool. Because of this piles can develop and the anus becomes sore and bleeding and a damp itching eruption ensues.

A fan-like motion of the nostrils is said to be a specific sign that Lycopodium is the remedy whatever the illness, but do not be put off using the remedy if this sign is not there if the symptoms fit in other ways.

Mentally the Lycopodium type is very intelligent, not just the kind of intelligence that is good at absorbing facts, but a thinker.

Sometimes the forehead is wrinkled giving them a concerned look, which isn't surprising as they can be anxious. One of the things they are anxious about is that they will not be able to accomplish anything, but when they come to do it they come up trumps and are surprised. There is a tendency to wake up in the morning with a 'fed up' feeling, but as the day wears on they become more optimistic, so they are often bad tempered first thing.

Contradiction can send them into a fury, for in any case they are easily annoyed and can be very irritable. The desire to be alone seems contradictory as they fear being alone. What they really want is to be alone in a house with somebody else in it.

There is a tendency to be over sensitive to pain to the point of frenzy, but I have to say that I have come across many Lycopodium types who are not particularly afflicted, and in some cases quite the reverse.

If they are annoyed about something they may not say anything, but does it show in their demeanour! It can range from bland disdain to a piercing glare, and though not exactly sulking they seem to have the ability to convey their displeasure by a distancing attitude.

The anxiety they suffer is more of an anticipation, usually about something that needs to be done. They can be talkative and fluent especially on a subject they know well, or an idea that they have had. Their ideas are not erratic like Sulphur, but well thought out and logical. When under stress they may have difficulty in expressing themselves and will use wrong words and pronunciations, even completely losing the thread of what they are saying.

NATRUM MURIATICUM

Physically these children tend to be on the small side for their age and underweight. Their backs are skinny and there is not much flesh round the collar bones. If the glands swell in the neck they will be small and hard like dried peas under the skin usually at the back of the neck.

They are chilly types and cannot do with draughts or extremes of temperature. Stuffy rooms do not agree with them and neither does the sun. If you are hoping for a happy holiday in Spain with these children then forget it, they will be miserable. Going out in the wind will make their eyes run, in fact they tend to make a lot of tears anyway.

Skin rashes seem to favour the hairline and forehead. The complexion has a pale fawn cast, and tends towards the greasy rather than being dry. In teenagers the greasiness becomes more pronounced, so they are bedevilled by blackheads and boils.

The skin round the nails is sensitive with cracks which are slow to heal and go septic. The bottom lip has a tendency to crack down the middle and sores or thrush are quite common. Have a look at the tongue which will look like crazy paving.

Headaches usually start after school age from concentrated mental effort, and though generally frontal with heaviness, they can be at the back of the head.

Mentally these types are not easy to spot in small children, but Nat. Mur. is a grand remedy in puberty. An outstanding symptom is the dislike of consolation when they are upset. It makes them furious – they prefer to be alone.

Small children dislike being handled and will cry more if you pick them up to comfort them.

Difficulty with articulation is noticeable in toddlers as they are slow talkers simply because they can't get their tongue round the words, and not through lack of comprehension. They know what they want to say but just find it difficult.

There is a tendency to be clumsy too, but really it is because they do things in too much of a hurry, and so become careless.

Older children are weepy and go off to have a little cry by themselves. If you are angry with them or chastise them they will appear not to bother, but you will hear them crying in their room; they do tend to be loners. When they are laughing it will often turn to tears, but not necessarily sad tears.

These are rather tense children, one might almost say they are rigid, and can be very critical and even quarrelsome. Small things annoy them, and their reaction is out of proportion. Taking umbrage is something they are good at, they will nurse small slights, mull over them, and take them out for an airing ages afterwards when one would think all was forgotten. There is a reluctance to tell their troubles in case they invoke sympathy which of course irritates them no end. If you ask them how they are they will automatically say they are very well when in fact are feeling lousy and then feel as though nobody cares.

After all this talk of irritability and sharp temper, oddly enough they can be very good company. There is however a possibility of depression, and it can be a very deep depression.

One of the things about young girls is that they tend to have crushes usually on some pimply youth, although it may be someone older like a teacher or a married man. When their attentions are not reciprocated or the object of their affections is patently unattainable, they will moon about and mope in their rooms and if pressed on the subject there will be hysterical outbursts.

Claustrophobia is a symptom of Nat. Mur. ranging from slight unease in lifts, crowded shops, or confined spaces right through to out and out panic.

When there is claustrophobia there is always a capability of being agoraphobic too and they will decide they don't want to go anywhere. Both these conditions can be present at the same time.

Sometimes there is a suspicion that intruders are in the house, and they will go round just to make sure in quite a calm manner. Arsen. Alb. is afraid of intruders but are much more agitated about it, and are great door lockers as they expect intruders to come, while Nat. Mur. thinks they are already there.

One last symptom which is peculiar to all age groups – they cannot pass urine if there is somebody else there, they must go to the bathroom alone, even toddlers are like this within their own family.

PHOSPHOROUS

Physically children of the Phosphorous type are thin with a narrow rib cage, and are rather weak – they need a lot of rest. In spite of this they never seem to be able to keep still, and are forever worming and fidgeting about. They have difficulty in getting to sleep before midnight so are consequently tired in the morning. Colds tend to settle on the chest and turn to bronchitis.

These children are prone to headaches which are congestive and throbbing. The headaches are much worse in the warmth, and are better for a cool atmosphere and cold compresses on the forehead. This is surprising as they dislike cold in other ways and want to be in warm rooms.

There is a need to eat often and they will become faint and shaky if deprived of the opportunity. Fond of salty foods and fats they will become flushed after a meal, particularly a hot meal. Cold drinks and ice cream are very much liked but don't suit them and will often make a small child sick. A snack in the night is something they are fond of if they can get the opportunity. There is a strong preference for lying on the right side to sleep.

Their sense of smell is acute and they are prone to nose bleeds, bright red blood will often be seen on the handkerchief after blowing the nose, particularly when they have a cold. Sensitivity to strong light, which they find very annoying, can bring on headaches.

Mentally they are bright, articulate, and very observant, although they do have difficulty at school because they tend to be forgetful, and of course feel tired most of the time so are unable to do their best. Co-ordination is quite good but they do seem to be 'butter-fingered'.

In class they appear to be sharp, talkative, and interested, yet their performance doesn't match up, so school reports will be of the 'intelligent but doesn't try' variety.

They are outgoing children who love to give and receive affection, and being very sympathetic, hate to see friends or family suffer or be upset. They rush forward to give comfort. They love company and hate to be alone, mainly I think because they like people so much.

They can be fearful, especially of thunder, and are rather nervy and excitable, often having tummy ache when they are afraid. It is worth remembering this when children complain of Monday morning tummy ache. It is not that they don't like school, since they are gregarious, but may be afraid of something, such as a teacher, the school bully, or even losing friends, as childrens' friendships are notoriously fickle.

PULSATILLA

Physically the Pulsatilla type is portrayed as fair, plump, female, and desperate for affection. Be not misled for there are plenty of darker, more spare and male Pulsatillas about.

These children hate hot weather even more than the Nat. Mur. type, it totally exhausts them. Cool air and cooler dry weather is what they really like, and their symptoms and temperament are better when these conditions prevail. Although they like cool weather it does tend to give them watery or sore eyes.

Hot stuffy rooms cannot be tolerated for any length of time as they may feel faint.

They can be great sufferers from earache, styes, cystitis, and ailments coming on from changes in the weather or getting wet.

The appetite is not particularly good, nor are they thirsty, but they do like rich foods such as fats, pastries, and ice cream. These foods however tend to give them indigestion or make them sick, as the digestive process is slow; although strangely enough butter seems to suit them.

Headaches, when they occur, are much better for a blow in the open air.

Symptoms of earache and catarrhal symptoms you will find in the appropriate places in this book. There is a tendency to dizziness when looking upwards, not often noticed in small children, probably because they can't express it. Pulsatilla types are said to sleep with the arms above the head and though often the case, I have come across many who do not.

Babies love being carried about and cuddled, and their crying sounds sad rather than angry. You get the impression that they are feeling neglected.

Mentally the Pulsatilla type is changeable. Although they appear to be sweet and loving, because they bask in love, there is if you look for it a streak of 'give it to me because I am so sweet'.

They cry when they are telling you how they feel, yet it can easily turn to laughter. Not quite the laughter of Nat. Mur., but a softer laughter that invites sympathy. As you laugh with them they are gaining from it.

This description sounds a little cynical I know, but their sweet and lovely exterior does belie the fact that they can be selfcentred, easily offended, and jealous. They want you to give them lots of affection and cuddles, but do not reciprocate in the way a Phosphorus child would do.

They are inclined to be nervous, afraid of being left alone, afraid of the dark, and shy. Bad dreams can occur after hearing or seeing unpleasant things. A bit lethargic during the day, they pick up later on and then have difficulty getting off to sleep.

This type does have a temper which flares up quickly and is just as quickly over. In fact they are as changeable as the weather. However they are on the whole placid, good tempered and not given to violence. The general impression is of a timid and hesitant child, but there can be undercurrents of discontent and misery.

Praise is very important for them, and there is a great need for approval. They really care what people think of them and generally try to please.

When at school they unfortunately can be easily led because they need the approval and acceptance of their peers. This can be very disconcerting for parents whose good little child suddenly gets into trouble having been carried along by their friends.

Being angry will be no help at all with this type of child, some constructive help and back up on how to say no will serve better.

They are conscientious at school, but cannot do their best because they are tired during the day time. There is no tendency to overwork as they are placid, but do try because of the need for approval.

Food fads are common, or they may decide certain foods are a bad thing and refuse to eat them. You could say there is an obsessive streak in their nature when they get these ideas.

Being rather imaginative as well as obsessive, there is always the possibility of being roped into some religious fad. This fortunately is quite rare, but one does hear of it happening from time to time.

SULPHUR

Sulphur has such a wealth of symptoms that one would think it covered every ailment, and there is no doubt that nearly everybody goes through a Sulphur phase at sometime during their life.

Dr Borland in his lectures on childrens' types describes two different types of sulphur child; the plump rosy type and the thinner, pale type.

The plump, well grown, rosy types perspire easily and have strong, thick hair. Their hands and face redden up when out in the cold and they also have a tendency to sore eyelids and poor eyelashes. Generally discontented and argumentative with a resentful attitude, they are also independent and will not tolerate help or advice. They appear lazy because they tire easily, even though they look so robust, and they are clumsy.

The thinner sulphur type has a poor physique, with thin legs, narrow chest and a big tummy. Vitality is lacking and they soon get low and weepy. Like Nat. Mur. when comforted they become irritated and snappy. Because of the lack of stamina they tire easily, and standing up for any length of time is impossible for them.

They are all hungry and love tasty foods, sweets, and some like fats but not all of them do. Curry and kippers and other such exotica go down well with toddlers when they won't touch ordinary plain dishes as one would expect. If they slosh sauce and condiments over everything – suspect sulphur.

Skin problems are prevalent of every variety imaginable. All sulphur skin eruptions are worse for warmth, particularly at night, and are worse for being washed. Like Calc. Carb. and Pulsatilla they will stick their feet out of bed at night to cool them down.

Even when there are no eruptions to be seen they can

itch when they get warm and they always feel better for a good scratch, even the eruptions feel better for scratching as there is temporary relief. Constipation can be stubborn, or alternatively there may be diarrhoea which comes on in the morning early and is burning, itching, and foul smelling.

Very often these children are sleepy and lazy during the day, especially after a meal, but become wakeful at night possibly with bad dreams. There is a tendency to become overheated, but not necessarily all over – they are more likely to feel hot in parts.

Much is made of the dislike of water or washing which is a particular symptom of Sulphur which is quite true, but is not always present. However there is no doubt that the skin eruptions are much worse for washing, and that there are some sulphur types who will avoid washing like the plague.

The same can be said of the drooping, ragged philosopher which is also very heavily quoted, but don't forget that Dr Borland's plump, rosy Sulphurs grow up, and look quite fresh and clean. Nor do they resemble the drooping theoriser who thinks he can mend the world by lying in a chair talking about it, although this type is the most common and most easily recognisable.

Mentally, on the whole, they are intelligent types, even given to strokes of genius, but their ideas are not consistent or well-thought-through. This type of mentality can be confusing for both parents and teachers, as one day they will produce excellent work, and hold meaningful conversations which display remarkable insight, but next day will be completely apathetic and quite dull.

These types are very easily offended, and can go off pop at the drop of a hat, or become resentful and badly done to. Everything he does or has he thinks better than anybody else's, even quite common and ordinary possessions. You will see this when a youngster says 'my Dad's car is the best' even when it is the most popular make around.

Teenagers who dress up in the most awful gear, look in the mirror and think they can see something wonderful are an example of this and surely need a dose of Sulphur. After a dose or two of Sulphur in these cases you will probably find you have uncovered the need for another remedy, but until you have got rid of that they will be an eternal mystery. At the other end of the scale there is the grubby, greasy looking outfit. Ill-assorted clothing and unwashed hair is the order of the day – do them a favour with a dose of Sulphur.

There is a selfishness in them too. They must have what they want when they want it, and they are certainly not prepared to wait for it without weeping and sulking. Even toddlers are like this, but some allowances must be made for the two to three age group who are trying to establish their identity.

They can become hypochondriacs, forgetful and worriers, in fact so low that they want to die. Drooping about is another irritating habit, they must lean on anything handy or lie about as everything is too much trouble except for thinking up impractical ideas.

5
Allergies

Allergies are a thorny problem and not easy to spot. There has been a great deal of controversy of late, with some people pooh-poohing the idea of food allergies altogether, while others have become obsessed. As usual, there is a middle road, but there is no doubt that allergies exist, and are becoming an increasing problem.

Many people think that allergic responses and intolerances are always very obvious. An example of this is hives after eating oranges, or a rash after eating strawberries, and oh! wouldn't it be nice if it were so simple. Unfortunately allergic responses can be quite insidious, with changing symptoms and a child who seems constantly under par.

As you will see from the reference to allergic coughs in the chapter on coughs, observation is the key to identifying allergy. The same applies to persistent tummy aches, bowel and digestive troubles if your child suffers from these. Usually the type of tummy ache is the same when it recurs indicating that the digestive system is the target for the allergy and the same goes for persistent sniffles and catarrh. I must stress again that children who have asthma and persistent respiratory problems are invariably allergic to some foods as well as dusts, pollens and hairs.

The skin scratch tests used in hospitals are notoriously inaccurate where foods are concerned, but are fairly reliable in diagnosing allergies to grasses, pollens, animal hairs, and dusts. Blood tests are much more accurate, but very expensive so are usually confined to use in specialist allergy clinics.

If food allergy is suspected, it may be worth changing the child's diet for a few weeks to see if there is any improvement, but do not expect to see much change in under three weeks. A word of caution here, do not cut out basic foods without replacing them with something equally nutritious.

An example of this is wheat. If you cut out wheat, make plain or sweet scones with other flours such as barley and soya mixed. Replace cane or beet sugar with fructose (fruit sugar), and cows' milk with soya or goats' milk. This will do no harm to the child, even if it does involve a little extra work. With regard to fruit juices, change from orange and blackcurrant to pineapple and grape, and so on.

I do find that vegetables other than potato are rarely a problem, and although occasionally they can be, vegetables are not the first place to look.

With regard to fruits, apples are a fruit that few parents ever suspect, but they contain salicylates which cause intolerances in some children, and of course any foods containing salicylates will have the same effect.

The immune system is not fully developed until the age of 12 years, which is why children seem to catch anything that is going in their early years. This is why, unless the child is really ill with infectious diseases, or coughs and colds, it is better to treat with natural methods wherever possible. Every time they have one of these ailments they are making antibodies to disease in the blood and so building up an immunity. To suppress the symptoms with unnecessary drugs is in the long run doing more harm than good as the immune process is interfered with.

You may wonder what this has to do with food. All foods are substances that are foreign to our bodies and we have a vast array of complicated mechanisms to deal with them; digestive processes, metabolism, and the immune system.

If all is working as it should there are no problems, if not symptoms begin to appear.

The allergic response is inflammatory, and it is this inflammation that develops in the weak places – the so-called 'target organs' – and causes the trouble.

This explanation is a very simple one, some would say too simple. Immunology is however a vast and complicated subject needing a book in itself, and I think a simple explanation is sufficient to make the problem clear.

Immunisation can put the immune system under great stress – it is one of my hobbyhorses but with good reason. Bearing in mind that the immune system in a baby is but poorly developed, and in the early months of life depends mainly on the immunity passed on through the mother's milk, it is small wonder that allergic problems start after the first immunisations. I have seen this happen too often to be passed off as coincidence. Immunisations contain foreign proteins which many babies just cannot cope with. My own feeling about this is that immunisation should not be given too early, and should not be administered as a triple vaccine, but singly.

The ravages of this practice can be modified by giving the baby 1 dose of Thuja 30 after every injection as soon as it comes home from the clinic. This will antidote the unwanted side effects of the vaccine, leaving the beneficial ones, and go a long way towards helping the baby to avoid allergic symptoms.

Another type of allergy is what is known as a masked allergy, which takes the form of an addiction. By this I mean that the child feels better for a short time after taking the particular food but this effect soon wears off and another 'fix' is needed. An example of this is sugar. The child is whining, tired, generally miserable, and may even have headaches. It rolls about the floor whingeing, snivelling and wanting sweeties. Give it a few sweeties and within a very short time you have a much happier, brighter child, more enthusiastic altogether. This happy state of affairs doesn't last long however as the whole process starts all over again.

Weaning a child off sugar is not an easy process but can be done if your nerves will stand it. Going 'cold turkey' is too traumatic for the mother, let alone the child. It is possible to make biscuits with fruit sugar, and they are nice dipped in carob or with dried fruit and carob chips baked in them. Get the child involved by allowing it to help make the biscuits. Frequent protein snacks instead of three set meals a day will help to keep the blood sugar up and cut down the craving. Dried fruit such as dates, figs, sultanas and raisins will also help as they have fruit sugar (fructose) in them. I am not suggesting that sugar as such is entirely bad for children, or that they should not have it, but it is unfortunately one of the most common masked allergies in children.

Candida Albicans (thrush) also has a bearing on allergic problems particularly if the mother has been plagued with this trouble over a long period; also persistant overdosing with antibiotics in early life.

Organic Brain Dysfunction (O.B.D.) can also put the child under stress. This dreadful sounding condition is a simple mechanical malfunction in co-ordination. It is usually caused by a very quick labour, a very long labour possibly with a forceps delivery, and in some cases after a caesarian section. Very high temperatures during the first year of life are also a predisposing factor. Simply this means that certain reflexes in the nervous system are not developed, or do not occur in the right order in the developing child. This gives rise to co-ordination difficulties akin to dyslexia with which it can be confused. There may be hyperactivity, hypersensitivity to noise and light, persistant crying, sleeplessness and even rocking and headbanging in infants. In older children the symptoms are more likely to be learning difficulties, hand to eye co-ordination poor, headaches associated with visual disorders, and clumsiness.

This condition can predispose the child to allergies because of the stress factor. Fortunately this condition can be rectified by an assessment of the extent of the problem, followed by a series of exercises tailored to suit the child.

Any form of stress can put an unacceptable burden on the immune system. By stress I am referring to such things as difficult births, long illnesses, family problems, surgical operations and difficulties at school.

I hope you will be able to cut down on the stress in your child's life by using this book to treat every day ailments and constitutional aberrations. If you can you will be doing your child, yourself and not least your doctor a favour.

6
Tips and Dosages

For beginners the safest potencies to use, unless otherwise stated in this book, are the 6th centesimal or the 30th centesimal potencies, normally sold in pharmacies labelled merely 6 and 30.

When giving the 6 potency in longstanding ailments give a dose 3 times daily between meals.

For acute conditions give a dose of the 6 potency every half hour for the first 6 doses followed by 3 times daily for one week unless there is improvement sooner, when no further medication is needed unless you are going to re-prescribe.

When using the 30 potency use one dose daily for 3 days and wait to assess results. Repeat at a later date only if the improvement is partial. In acute cases give 3 doses in the day only.

When using the 200 or 1M potency give one dose only and do not repeat for at least three weeks, and then only if there has been improvement but only partial success. This is because it is not necessary to repeat the medicine, as it keeps on working in the higher potencies without repetition, and to repeat too soon may spoil the action of the remedy.

In skin problems when treating at home never give a potency higher than 6 in case of aggravations of the symptoms. If the 6 potency has done some good and then stops working it can repeated in the 30 potency, then wait and repeat again when necessary.

After antibiotics give Nux Vomica 6, one dose daily for 7 days, as it helps to clear the system of their unwanted side effects.

After immunisation give Thuja 30 one dose only, again to get rid of unwanted side effects.

To boost the immune system at any time give Lachesis 6 one dose daily for 7 days.

After surgery give Phosphorous 30 one dose only to antidote the effects of the anaesthetic, and one dose of Hypericum 30 for the wounds.

After shock and bruising give Arnica 30 one dose, or Aconite 30, one dose for shock alone.

After head injuries or concussion give Nat. Sulph. 30 one dose and possibly Arnica 30 one dose, if there is bruising.

Homoeopathic remedies can safely be given along with medication from your G.P. when this has been absolutely necessary. This will not interfere with the treatment given by your doctor, although drugs will interfere with the efficacy of the homoeopathic remedies in that they will not be as successful.

Whenever possible do not suppress the development of pus by constantly giving antibiotics in cases of acne in teenagers as this can lead to nervous disorders. Take the patient to a herbalist or homoeopath whenever possible. Very often if you can find the constitutional remedy and give it there will be a great deal of improvement.

Do have antibiotics in cases of ear infection or tooth abcesses in children and then correct the residual effects of these afterwards.

When in any doubt as to the diagnosis of the illness take the child to your G.P. It is all too easy to become an overenthusiastic amateur homoeopath and it could be dangerous if you have missed vital clues, particularly in cases of abdominal pain.

It is best to try and work with your doctor at all times. Many doctors these days are interested in other therapies, and would like to know more about them, so you will find that most will go along with you even if it be a little bit tongue in cheek in some cases.

Suggested Further Reading

Children's Types, Douglas M. Borland – London: British Homoeopathic Association

Common Ailments of Children and Their Homoeopathic Management, M.T. Santwani – New Delhi: Jain Publishing Co.

Homoeopathic Drug Pictures, M.L. Tayler – Saffron Walden: Health Science Press.

Homoeopathic Remedies for Children, Phyllis Speight – Saffron Walden: Health Science Press.

Studies of Homoeopathic Remedies, Douglas Gibson – Beaconsfield: Beaconsfield Publishers Ltd.

Everyday Homoeopathy, David Gemmell – Beaconsfield: Beaconsfield Publishers Ltd.

Introduction to Homoeopathic Medicine, Hamish W. Boyd – Beaconsfield: Beaconsfield Publishers Ltd.

Homoeopathic Remedies for Womens' Ailments, Phyllis Speight – Saffron Walden: Health Science Press.

Not all in the Mind, Richard Mackarness – London: Pan Books.

Chemical Victims, Richard Mackarness – London: Pan Books.

Allergies and the Hyperactive Child, Doris J. Rapp – New York: Cornerstone Library.

Useful Addresses

British Homoeopathic Association, 27a Devonshire Street, London W1N 1RJ.

Hahnemann Society, Humane Education Centre, Bounds Green Road, London N22 4EU.

Homoeopathic Development Foundation, Harcourt House, 19aCavendish Square, London W1M 9AD.

Society of Homoeopaths (Register of Homoeopaths), 2 Artisan Road, Northampton NN1 4HU.

Institute for Neurophysiological Psychology (For OBD treatment), 4 Stanley Place, Chester, Cheshire.

Institute of Allergy Therapists (Register of Allergists), Llangwyryfon, Aberystwyth, Dyfed.

Donald M. Harrison B.A.(Hons), B.Sc., M.P.S. (Homoeopathic Chemist), Fynnonwen Natural Therapy Centre, Llangwyryfon, Aberystwyth.

National Institute of Medical Herbalists, 41 Hatherley Road, Winchester, Hants.

Ainsworth's (Homoeopathic Chemists), 38 New Cavendish Street, London W1M 7HL.

Nelsons (Homoeopathic Chemists), 73 Duke Street, London W1.

Sheila Harrison R.G.N., Ffynnonwen Natural Therapy Centre, Llangwyryfon, Aberystwyth.